LEONARD J. ARRINGTON
MORMON HISTORY LECTURE SERIE
No. 16

A Mountain of Paper
The Extraordinary Diary oi Leonard James Arrington

by

Carl Arrington and

Susan Arrington Madsen

.

September 23, 2010

Sponsored by

Special Collections & Archives
Merrill-Cazier Library
Utah State University
Logan, Utah

ISBN 978-0-87421-846-6 (paper)
ISBN 978-0-87421-847-3 (e-book)

Distributed by
Utah State University Press
Logan, Utah 84322-3078

Foreword

F. Ross Peterson

The establishment of a lecture series honoring a library's special collections and a donor to that collection is unique. Utah State University's Merrill-Cazier Library houses the personal and historical collection of Leonard J. Arrington, a renowned scholar of the American West. As part of Arrington's gift to the university, he requested that the university's historical collection become the focus for an annual lecture on an aspect of Mormon history. Utah State agreed to the request and in 1995 inaugurated the annual Leonard J. Arrington Mormon History Lecture.

Utah State University's Special Collections and Archives is ideally suited as the host for the lecture series. The state's land grant university began collecting records very early, and in the 1960s became a major depository for Utah and Mormon records. Leonard and his wife Grace joined the USU faculty and family in 1946, and the Arringtons and their colleagues worked to collect original diaries, journals, letters, and photographs.

Although trained as an economist at the University of North Carolina, Arrington became a Mormon historian of international repute. Working with numerous colleagues, the Twin Falls, Idaho, native produced the classic *Great Basin Kingdom: An Economic History of the Latter-day Saints* in 1958. Utilizing available collections at USU, Arrington embarked on a prolific publishing and editing career. He and his close ally, Dr. S. George Ellsworth, helped organize the Western History Association, and they created the *Western Historical Quarterly* as the scholarly voice of the WHA. While serving with Ellsworth as editor of the new journal, Arrington also helped both the Mormon History Association and the independent journal *Dialogue* get established.

One of Arrington's great talents was to encourage and inspire other scholars or writers. While he worked on biographies or institutional histories, he employed many young scholars as researchers. He fostered many careers as well as arranged for the publication of numerous books and articles.

In 1973, Arrington accepted appointments as the official historian of the Church of Jesus Christ of Latter-day Saints and the Lemuel Redd Chair of Western History at Brigham Young University. More and more Arrington focused on Mormon, rather than economic, historical topics. His own career flourished with the publication of *The Mormon Experience*, co-authored with Davis Bitton, and *American Moses: A Biography of Brigham Young*. He and his staff produced many research papers and position papers for the LDS Church as well. Nevertheless, tension developed over the historical process, and Arrington chose to move full time to BYU with his entire staff. The Joseph Fielding Smith Institute of History was established, and Leonard continued to mentor new scholars as well as publish biographies. He also produced a very significant two-volume study, *The History of Idaho*.

After Grace Arrington passed away, Leonard married Harriet Horne of Salt Lake City. They made the decision to deposit the vast Arrington collection of research documents, letters, files, books, and journals at Utah State University. The Leonard J. Arrington Historical Archives is part of the university's Special Collections. The Arrington Lecture Committee works with Special Collections to sponsor the annual lecture.

About the Authors

Carl Arrington, the second son (middle child) of Leonard and Grace Arrington, was born in Logan, Utah in 1951. He grew up in Cache Valley attending Adams Elementary, Logan Junior High (where he was suspended for publishing the underground newspaper the *Buffalo Bull*) and Logan High, where he was a debater and the editor of the *Grizzly*. He attended Utah State University where he was elected sophomore class president, published *The Aggie Joker* humor magazine, and wrote a column for *Student Life*. He also dated an unseemly number of beautiful sorority girls and served proudly-though-meekly as an Alpha Chi Omega "Worm." As a USU freshman Carl took the History of Economic Thought class taught by his professor father. He got an "A," but claims there was "NO nepotist favoritism." (R-i-i-i-ight...) He earned a BA from USU in 1975 with double majors in political science and journalism.

A somewhat more pious version of Carl (which has since mysteriously dissipated) served an LDS mission to Bolivia where he dined on sheep's head soup and survived the Banzer Revolution. Later as an intern at the Mormon youth magazine *The New Era* in 1974, he invented the "MormonAd." He also worked for his father as a researcher at the Historical Department of the LDS Church during the four minutes that "Camelot" lasted.

During the time of the Watergate hearings in Washington, D.C., Carl worked on Capital Hill as a congressional aide in the press office of Rep. Dick Shoup (R-Mont.), but then happily gave up politics for rock and roll. As a reporter and rock critic Carl worked for the *Detroit Free Press* and the *New York Post*. He was managing editor for the hard rock magazine *Circus* and for eight years was a correspondent, critic, and editor *at People Magazine* where he wrote many cover profiles of such celebrities as Madonna, Tina Turner, Sylvester Stallone and Michael Jackson. He also reported the story about the Mark Hoffman bombings. He was a radio commentator for the CBS Radio Network. He has also written for *Time, Rolling Stone, Creem, Friends, Us Weekly, TV Guide, New Age, USA Weekend* and other popular magazines.

In Los Angeles, Carl worked for several years as a movie critic for the website Entertainment Asylum and then as managing news editor of the Internet portal Entertaindom. Carl proudly appeared on stage as a "monk" during the mock-execution of a midget during the finale of an Ozzy Osbourne concert at Nassau Coliseum in New York.

Carl has two daughters, Alexis and Olivia. He currently works as a freelance writer and media consultant. He lives in New York City.

Susan Arrington Madsen grew up in Logan where she graduated from Utah State University with a degree in journalism. During her years at USU, she was awarded an internship with LDS Church Magazines, wrote for the USU student newspaper as a senior staff writer, and wrote over forty articles for *Collier's Encyclopedia Yearbooks*.

Although it was too late to take an economics class from her father, Susan did take a music class from Dean Madsen, USU's most eligible bachelor. She later commented, "If I had worked as hard in my other courses as I did in that music class, I would have been valedictorian of my college. But I didn't, and so I wasn't." She and Dean have been married now for thirty-six years, the parents of four daughters, and the grandparents of eleven beloved grandchildren.

Susan has published nine books, several of which have to do with women and children in Mormon pioneer history. Her bestseller can probably be found in the home libraries of many Mormons, the title being *I Walked to Zion: True stories of Young Pioneers On the Mormon Trail.*

In addition to her publishing career, Susan has contributed to the communities in her much-loved Cache Valley. She served as a member of the Cache County School District Board of Education for six years, she was on the Hyde Park Board of Adjustments for nine years, and was awarded the National Daughters of Utah Pioneers Community Service Award.

Dean and Susan recently served as a "Service Couple" in Tiberias, Israel, living in an LDS Church-owned facility just a stone's throw from the Sea of Galilee. While there, they taught English at an all-girls' Arab/Christian High School in Nazareth, Dean taught music and directed a music ensemble at a private Catholic High School, also in Nazareth, and they conducted twenty oral interviews of members of the LDS faith in northern Israel.

A Mountain of Paper:
The Extraordinary Diary of Leonard James Arrington

Introduction

A Soldier in Rome

CARL: At the end of World War II, an American soldier stationed in Rome went to visit Roman Catholic sites on his day off. This Private First Class from Idaho, with some purpose in mind, found his way to the majestic Basilica of St. John Lateran, which is famous as the place where Roman Catholic Popes are crowned while sitting upon an ancient bronzed throne. The brash young soldier went straight to the apse to gaze upon this gleaming seat of ecclesiastic power. What the young soldier did next we know because of what he wrote on the back of a picture-postcard of the papal seat of power. "When the guard wasn't looking," recounts the soldier, "I lifted the barrier rope, climbed the stairs, and sat on the throne!"

SUSAN: The only reason we know that God did *not* smite this soldier is because this young man was our father, Leonard James Arrington, and he lived to tell about it.

Leonard's Legacy—Why We Are Here Tonight

SUSAN: Tonight we are gathered in this historic Tabernacle to celebrate the life of Leonard Arrington and the official opening of his diary. We are grateful to have been asked to share our enthusiasm and gratitude for this remarkable document, which is written by, and about, this stalwart saint, scholar, and mentor.

CARL: One of the brightest minds and insightful experts of the modern LDS Church is Greg Prince, who co-wrote the recent award-winning biography of President David O. McKay. He makes the following assessment of the diary's importance:

> The Arrington diary was written (and compiled) entirely by Leonard (J.) Arrington. We know the mind and soul of Leonard, because *he* placed

them on the page. ...The opening of the Arrington diary to the public is one of the most significant events in Mormon historiography in decades. Generations of researchers, writers, and readers will be the richer for Leonard's almost unbelievable devotion to diary writing, and (for) the commitment of the Arrington family and Utah State University to make the diaries accessible.

We are happy to inform you all that Greg is hard at work on a biography of our father. The family is thrilled.

SUSAN: So, what brings all of you here tonight? Perhaps you attend this Lecture Series because you believe Mormon history and the history of the American West are important, and you are eager to learn more. Perhaps you come because Leonard was your professor at USU or BYU. Maybe you knew Leonard as a colleague in the LDS Church Historical Department. You might be here because he changed your life as a result of an unplanned conversation you had with him on an airplane, at a lecture he gave, or in his office. There are many who fit that description.

CARL: Leonard Arrington touched lives and wrote histories that permeate just about every facet of life here in the Beehive State. If you have a job at Hill Field, or Thiokol, or at the Bingham Kennecott Copper Mine, or if you are a sugar beet farmer, Leonard has probably written about your company, your family, or your college. Maybe, in fact, he has written about *you*.

SUSAN: Maybe you never met Leonard Arrington, but are a fan of his books. He wrote, co-authored, or contributed to thirty-six books and twenty-two monographs during his lifetime. Perhaps you read his definitive biography of Brigham Young, or his insightful explanation of Mormon culture in *Mormon Experience*, which he co-authored with his great friend Davis Bitton. Maybe you read his grand-slam book published in 1958, *Great Basin Kingdom: An Economic History of the Latter-day Saints, 1830–1900*, which today is recognized as the definitive book written about the settlement of the Intermountain West. It remains in print, fifty-two years after it first appeared.

This evening we are not merely recounting the strides Leonard and his fellow historians have made in creating the New Mormon History. We are here to celebrate the life of a man who was dynamic, thoughtful, prayerful, and surely one of the best listeners ever born to woman. He was indeed something of a father-confessor to hundreds, who came to him to speak of things about which they'd spoken to no other. He was one of the most tolerant, non-judgmental, and sympathetic souls you might encounter. This Tabernacle probably would not hold the number of closet doubters who came to Leonard seeking wisdom, and found it.

CARL: We believe that our father's diary will come to be known as one of the most astonishing documents held by Utah State University Special Collections. Leonard not only lived a very interesting life, he was a diarist and, boy, did he ever have a lot to write about! Those few minutes spent writing practically every day, or at least once a week, grew to be a thirty-thousand-page diary by the time Dad passed away. It occupies twenty-six linear feet on the shelves in USU Special Collections.

Leonard's diary includes his earliest autobiographical notes, which he started writing in 1927, at the age of ten, as a farm boy in Idaho. It continues through his public school years, through his undergraduate studies at the University of Idaho, his graduate studies at the University of North Carolina in Chapel Hill, and on through the twenty-six years he spent as an esteemed and monstrously productive Aggie professor. It covers his profound and influential service as Church Historian for The Church of Jesus Christ of Latter-day Saints, and records his thoughts, feelings, and accomplishments during his post-retirement years, up until twelve days before he passed away.

SUSAN: In addition to reading about Dad's daily or weekly activities, a researcher in the library opening a folder containing a portion of his diary will also find thank-you notes galore, Happy Birthday cards, tickets to an opera he attended and loved, newspaper obituaries of people with whom he had some kind of connection, as well as invitations, magazine articles, political cartoons, and editorials of interest. Oh yes, there is one other item you will see. Each year, my father photocopied and placed in his diary his current Temple Recommend. There is certainly a message in that.

CARL: Thanks to Dad's passion for record keeping, especially for keeping his own personal diary, we have a mountain of paper, a mountain of words Dad wrote for us, for you, for anyone interested. And to fulfill that purpose, Dad entrusted his diary to Utah State University, along with his vast personal library of over ten thousand books and 639 archival boxes full of research on every topic imaginable. Also included in his collection are his hundreds of speeches and his voluminous file of correspondence. Dad loved Utah State, and the surest proof of his love is that his diary is here.

Leonard's Birth and Boyhood

CARL: The world little Leonard arrived in was an embattled world. The Great War—as World War I was known at the time—raged in Europe. Leonard James Arrington was born July 2, 1917, in a small frame home on the outskirts of Twin Falls, Idaho. He was the second son and the third child of Edna Grace Corn Arrington and Noah Wesley Arrington. Both of Leonard's parents were Mormon converts, back when the total Church membership was less than five hundred thousand.

Illnesses

CARL: The Arringtons' lives were precarious, and certain dangers swept down on tiny Leonard in a Stephen King-worthy cataract of medical calamities. As an infant and toddler, Dad survived typhoid fever, small pox and surgery to remove his tonsils. Leonard's diary tells of his closest brush with death:

> In January 1919, I became ill with influenza and within a few days [it] developed into pneumonia.

Just a reminder that this Great Flu Epidemic killed ten times more people than died in World War I and is still considered the most deadly epidemic since the Black Plague, which wiped out one-third of Europe in the mid-1300s. Back to Leonard.

> I came very near passing away, since my mother and father were sick at the same time …When Doctor Cloucheck knew I had pneumonia, he told my father, who was also down with the flu, that I would die within 24 hours. My father seemed resigned to my death, having previously lost a daughter, Thelma, to spinal meningitis. But my mother was not willing to accept that possibility. She got up, over the strong objections of the doctor, and joined Sister Bowen in anointing me, blessing me, and praying for me. Their blessing was efficacious and of course I survived … My mother always believed that God had saved me for a special purpose. As I achieved in school, and in other activities, she believed I was vindicating God's saving gift to her.

SUSAN: That experience, that miraculous healing as a result of an anointing and prayer from two faithful women not only saved his life but it had a profound impact on my father in at least two ways. It helps explain, for me, why my father had such great respect for women in the

LDS Church. He was one of the first Mormon historians to recognize the astonishing contributions women made to almost every aspect of the settling of the Utah Territory—their heavy workload both inside and outside of their homes; their service in medicine, politics, and literature; and their service as schoolmarms and midwives.

A Sense of Destiny Confirmed

CARL: His miraculous survival also helps to explain why Leonard, from infancy on, seemed to have such a sure sense of purpose, even as he faced danger and adversity. He had a sturdy personal conviction inside that he truly had a personal destiny. That sense of purpose began quite humbly, yet doggedly. It surely provided some of the fire in his belly that took him through the challenges that lay ahead; it helped make him a powerful mentor and a valiant friend of the truth.

Leonard the Public School Student

CARL: In 1923 a new era began for young Leonard. He started school.

> When six years old, I started school in Twin Falls. I enrolled in Washington School in [the] first grade. On the report cards my parents received, my grades were "Very Goods" and "Excellents."

Father Noah Called to Serve a Mission

CARL: And then came a huge life-altering challenge for the small, struggling Arrington farm family with four children, each under the age of ten.

> In December 1924, my father got notice from [the Church] in Salt Lake [City], saying he was called to go on a mission to the Southern States. We had to move into a house next to two of my uncles' and grandpa's [house]. Daddy left for Atlanta, Georgia, January 7, 1925. This left Mamma, LeRoy, and I to do the work on the farm. I also got a job helping my uncles in the dairy for 35 cents a Day.

Oh, yes, one more thing to add to the challenging situation—Mother Edna was five months pregnant with another child.

Pure Hard Work as a Chicken Farmer and Business Man

CARL: With his father more than a thousand miles away, and a farm to run, Leonard blossomed as an entrepreneur. He explains how it started:

> One day when I didn't have anything to do, a chicken seller came to our place. He said he had some prize-winning Wyandotte hens that laid 300 eggs in 365 days, and also some prize-winning roosters. So, I bought a dozen hens and a rooster. The next thing to do was to build a chicken coop. First I made four post holes, and built the coop allowing three square feet for each chicken.

Eight-year old Leonard goes on to provide detailed instructions for the building of the chicken coop. So, Leonard became a chicken farmer, giving him work that became an important source of food and also an important cash crop for the family. This was not some passing summer hobby. Leonard stuck with it over the years. He joined the Future Farmers of America and, naturally, used chickens as his livestock project. Leonard writes of what the bottom line was at the end of this new adventure:

> My beginning inventory amounted to $35.50 and at the end of my project, its value was $824.25.

Okay, investors, that is a profit of more than 2,000 *percent!* And besides that, if any of you have questions about whether Leonard Arrington was a true intellectual, from this story you can, at least, no longer dispute that he truly was a *wildly successful egg-head!*

Spelling
SUSAN: As Leonard continued his elementary school education, his special skills as a gifted student manifested themselves early.

> During my fifth year of school … I studied very hard, getting high grades. I specialized in spelling, missing only THREE WORDS that [whole] year… In sixth grade I [also] worked quite hard with my studies. I took a special interest in History, and [again in] Spelling. Our room had a spelling match, and I stayed up the longest.

Leonard's fascination with reading and spelling continued. On March 18,1931, the great Magic Valley County Spelling Bee was held:

> We spelled [for] two hours before a girl from Filer, [Idaho], named Helen Williams, won. We spelled 108 words before I missed the wretched word "reimburse," spelling it "r-e-e-m-b-e-r-c-e." I had never heard of [the word] before.

Farm Work and Reading the Scriptures

CARL: But Leonard's life wasn't all spelling bees and school work. His responsibilities on the farm, and his personal reading, continued.

> That summer of 1929 I worked very hard, harrowing, clod-mashing, weeding beans, watering, and night-shading.

SUSAN: Shortly after he was ordained a deacon at age twelve, he writes about his reading:

> We had been studying the Bible in Sunday School, so I started reading it for myself. I started [on] June 6, 1930, and after eight months of every-day reading, I finished [on] February 6, 1931.

That is about nine pages, or 3,429 words, every day for this thirteen-year-old boy. I am not sure anyone would call Leonard a "pious" individual, but he kindled in himself a fire of interest in religion.

Youth Genealogy Class and Writing Family History

SUSAN: In 1929, under the guidance and inspiration of Leonard's Aunt Callie, the Twin Falls Ward innovated the *first* junior genealogical class that we know of in the Church:

> On November 10, 1929, at 8:00 a.m., was the first meeting [of the genealogical class] … Our first project was to fill out a pedigree chart for ourselves. The second was to fill out a family group sheet for our family. The third project was to write our own life history. They even instructed us how to do this. We were to begin as Nephi of old did, "I, Nephi, having been born of goodly parents," and so on.

And indeed the first words of Leonard's diary that we are celebrating this evening, are, "I, Leonard, having been born of goodly parents…." Thus he commenced his Book of Remembrance, and started researching the family's history by writing letters to relatives and interviewing them to get dates and other information on his family.

> I shall always be grateful for having had the opportunity of participating in this Family History program. It proved of enormous value to me, and our family.

A College Education

CARL: Growing out of these youthful experiences, Leonard chose to do something that no other member of the Arrington family had yet done—that was to enroll in a university and acquire a college education.

Father Noah disapproved, saying he would gladly support Leonard in serving a mission for the Church, but could offer no financial help for college. Noah even declined to let Leonard use the money Leonard had built up from his chicken and egg business for college expenses.

Undaunted, Leonard enrolled at the University of Idaho in Moscow, where he supported himself with scholarships, by working as a hasher in the university eating hall, and by working on farms, shoveling—as he put it—"gold dust" (meaning cow manure) to pay his way. Leonard had this to say about his decision to study at the university:

> I thought I could serve the Church and Kingdom by getting a good education. I didn't understand why the Church couldn't give recognition for missionary service to people who studied, and wrote, and taught the Gospel, in the context of higher learning. I felt a strong sense of mission in my schoolwork and felt the need to continue.

SUSAN: And continue he did. He studied, worked, and prayed hard during the challenging voyage of his freshman year. At the end of that school year, in 1936, he took account of himself in his diary:

> A great change occurred in my spiritual attitude [since going to college]. This change may be for good or for bad—I don't know. Many comparisons can be made between my former and present attitude(s). One [part of that change] is in toleration. I used to hate people that smoked tobacco. Today, some of my best friends smoke. I used to hate people that drank liquor. Today, I hate only the liquor; and I pity the people who overuse it. I used to think that every statement in the Bible was inspired and faultless. I used to think that all of the other churches were wrong and that only mine was right. Having visited other churches, and having become acquainted with people of other denominations, I realize that there is good and bad in every religion, but mostly good in all of them.

Leonard finished his bachelor's degree at the University of Idaho. Clearly, he was growing, becoming a new and deeper person.

North Carolina Studies, Marriage, Army Service, and USU

SUSAN: After completing his studies at the University of Idaho, Leonard worked on his PhD at the University of North Carolina. There he met and married a lovely Southern belle, Grace Fort. They were married in the Hayes Barton Baptist Church in 1943, just one week before he shipped out as an Army soldier for what turned out to be three years of service in the European theater of World War II.

Leonard and Grace wrote letters to each other daily—and I do mean *daily*—over a span of three years, for a total of more than six thousand pages! Leonard served honorably as an enlisted corporal in the United States Army, serving mostly in the battle theaters and in the American-run prisoner of war camps in North Africa.

He also served in Italy, where, among other things, he became fascinated with Italian opera and, as we mentioned before, contrived to sit upon the precious papal throne in Rome.

Army Life, and a Love Poem for Grace

SUSAN: In a letter to Grace, who was living in Raleigh where she and her mother ran a beauty shop, Leonard describes his army quarters in North Africa, and then goes on to something much more important:

> I look about me. Within three feet of me now, is everything I own in Africa. At my feet, to the side, is one barracks bag. Hanging on a nail over-head is another—both chocked full. I'm sitting on my bed, [up]on which are my helmet, [a] field jacket – [and] an overcoat for [a] pillow. In front to the right is the big box in which I have my books, your letters, cans of milk, chocolate, chewing gum, and scissors. In front of me is our G.I. water can. [These things are] what I see about me when I'm [being] realistic.
>
> Next to the wall, is your picture. When I go outside to look at the moon and stars—to hold communion with God—I seem to be in another world. The Arabian smells, the [Arabs] arguing, the arguing of [the] Italians, the shattered buildings, and [the] ack-ack nests, all fade out of existence. It seems as though you're looking at me, soft and lovingly.

And then Leonard waxes romantic and pens this poem for his wife, Grace:

> I would not change you in any single way.
>
> The steadfast dream I've held through years long gone

Is realized completely now in you.

You are the answer to my prayer,

The vision in my heart.

Your voice is the golden melody of dreamland,

Your eyes as clear as springtime lakes.

Oh, my darling, how I wish I could love you now!

...Your adoring husband, Jimmie.

Family Life in Utah

SUSAN: After the war, Leonard returned to finish his PhD in North Carolina. In 1946, he and Grace "crossed the plains" to Utah in an automobile they named "Mr. Bill." Leonard joined the faculty of Utah State University in Logan, where he held the position of Professor of Economics for twenty-six years. We lived most of the time in Logan, but also lived two years in Los Angeles and a year in Italy. We were an adventurous, literary, rambunctious, and welcoming family.

Our Arrington household had many overnight house guests. We had grandmothers, uncles, strange aunts, rapscallion cousins, renowned scholars, chums, foreign exchange students, and even some surprise visitors. Some more surprising than others. The summer after I graduated from Logan High School, I moved to Salt Lake City with my parents. I was working the late shift at a burger joint and came home late after everyone else had gone to bed. As I turned on the light in my bedroom, what should appear in my bed but a very large and hairy man! As they say on TV, "*awk-ward!*" I'm not sure whether it was my terrified *gasp!* or the very unexpected man's grizzled "*whaaahh?*" which brought my Father quickly to the scene to clarify the situation before any karate chops were delivered.

In fact the man with the dark beard was a brilliant scholar, a Korean War veteran, and the great-great-great (and I do mean *great*) grandson of the Prophet Joseph Smith. The man I discovered in my bed—who is now seventy-seven and, from all reports, still handsomely hairy—was none other than Paul M. Edwards, a distinguished member of the faculty of Graceland College and one of the brilliant friends that my father fostered among the members of the RLDS church.

New Year's Eve Family Meetings
SUSAN: Reflecting on our family life, one of the most charming records to be found in Dad's diary are the "minutes" of our annual family New Year's Eve meetings which began in 1966. We held them annually for more than thirty years.

One of the things we did was create revealing "Favorites Lists." Dad's astonishing list of things he liked best reveals the complexity of his tastes. From some of his choices he seems very cultured—even high-brow—when he identifies Beethoven's Ninth Symphony as his favorite music and Santiago's *Life of Reason* as his favorite book. Perhaps it is no surprise that he identified Brigham Young was his favorite personality. But this sublime list was not without the ridiculous. His favorite Beatles song was "We All Live in a Yellow Submarine" and his two favorite TV programs were wacky military spoofs, "McHale's Navy," and "Hogan's Heroes." Watching these shows, dad laughed until he cried!

Leonard's Spontaneity
CARL: Leonard loved corny jokes and spontaneous social behavior. He was not above pointing out the window saying, "Look! It's a rare red-winged blackbird!" and while everyone was looking outside he would use the opportunity to pick up his plate and lick it clean of boysenberry pancake syrup.

Leonard Was Saved by Grace
CARL: We need to say loud and clear that Leonard was "Saved By Grace." The reason he had time to be the most prolific scholar in the West was because of our mother, Grace. She was a dynamo, taking care of the house and yard, raising the three children, buying and cooking the food. She also designed and oversaw the building of our house in Logan, at 810 North 400 East. Those seventy foot trees that are there today were planted by my mother and me.

If Leonard Arrington is the father of Mormon Studies, we guarantee that Grace Arrington is their mother. Leonard's sole job was that of provider and Grace did the rest. When Grace added Italian delicacies to the usual menu that included killer Southern Fried everything, our table was a magnet for strays, aspiring girlfriends, and our beloved Nana. But Leonard helped in his own way. When I needed a printing press to run off an underground newspaper in junior high school, Dad supplied the printing press. He was an organizer and intervened for truth and justice in a myriad of ways, from writing letters of recommendation, to helping a friend out of a tight spot with a loan.

Leonard's Weekly Family Letters

SUSAN: Big changes in our family life took place in 1972, when Dad was called to be the Church Historian. My parents moved from Logan to Salt Lake City. My brother James was studying at the American Conservatory Theater in San Francisco. Carl was on a mission in Bolivia. I was a freshman at USU.

With a suddenly empty nest, Dad started writing a weekly family letter to keep in touch with us and to share, in detail, his and our goingson. He sent the same letter to the three of us, using carbon paper in his manual typewriter. With his legendary consistency, Dad hardly missed writing a family letter every week from 1972 to the week before he died, in February of 1999. That is twenty-seven years worth of weekly family letters!

Leonard's Phenomenal Memory

CARL: Everywhere Leonard went, he took his amazing memory with him. While a professor at USU, he also served on a stake high council and in a stake presidency. I remember when he was on the high council he would be assigned to go speak in some far-flung Cache Valley ward like Cornish or Cove or Avon. After the meeting, it seemed inevitable that some young person would say "hello" to Leonard and introduce him or herself. Then Leonard would often say something like:

> Oh, so your name is Utahna Lawanna Larsen. I see.

Leonard would then pause for a dramatic moment, like a mind-reader, somewhat like Carnac, and then continue with a flourish:

> Oh, you must be from the Sven Olaf Jenson Hanson Swenson Larsen pioneer family from Scandinavia! Their travel was financed by the Perpetual Emigration Fund! They came across the plains in 1857, and entered the Valley about August 19th. [Pause] Let's see, my recollection has it that they had jerky, fried bread, and butter, for their first meal in the Salt Lake Valley. [Pause] Oh yes! And I believe your great-great-great-great grandfather was wearing a brown hat at the time of that meal!

By this time the shocked young person would have their eyes wide open, and their jaw on the floor, as they listened to this friendly stranger accurately describe, in minute detail, their pioneer family history.

Leonard often knew more about your family than *you* did. Don't feel bad if this actually happened to you. It happened to almost *everybody* he met in the whole Great Basin Kingdom. It was actually scary how much Leonard Arrington knew. The truth is, if a fact was knowable and within fifty feet of Leonard, he knew it.

Leonard's Calling, Service, Experiences, and Accomplishments as Church Historian

CARL: As mentioned previously, in 1972, Leonard was called by President Joseph Fielding Smith to be the Church Historian and Recorder. In our minds, and in the minds of many others, he became truly a model Church Historian for all to emulate. Arrington, with a crack team of professional young historians, revolutionized Mormon Studies. Wisely, the team was given full access to the vast Church Archives. Leonard also founded the Mormon History Association, and was a founding advisor for *Dialogue: The Journal of Mormon Thought.*

The History Division of the Church was also created in 1972 with Leonard as director. The division was charged with responsibility to conduct research and writing projects on behalf of the Church. It flourished under Leonard's leadership for a decade, from 1972 to 1982. During that time-span, members of the History Division staff published fifteen books with six others well under way; published more than four hundred articles in professional journals, Church magazines, and other article series; and recorded some fifteen hundred oral history interviews with seven hundred and fifty persons in multiple languages. All of this helped take Mormon history to a new level.

Leonard's Comments on General Conference Sessions

SUSAN: Leonard attended General Conference for many years before, during, and after his service as Church Historian. When he received his calling, one of the advantages he enjoyed was reserved seating near the front of the congregation in the Tabernacle on Temple Square. In his diary, he regularly made interpretive comments about the people he met, the seating arrangements for Church leaders, the spirit and personal meaning of the talks given, and many other aspects of the general conference of the Church. Here is one example reflecting his strong opinion on the seating of the presidencies of the women's auxiliaries:

> The women presidencies . . . sit near the front on the farthest right side facing the stand. Why couldn't those sisters be placed in the center [section of the congregation], behind the regional representatives and in front of stake presidents? Why do they have to be shunted over to the far right? Or, why not find a place for the three presidents—Relief Society, Young Women, and Primary—on the stand or [on the] front row? Another thing that must seem peculiar to some observers is that all of the special guests on the first two rows all the way across [the congregation in] the Tabernacle, are men. Don't we ever have any special guests who are women? If not, why not?

CARL: It is no secret that Leonard had among LDS leaders friends, enemies, and even—as Perez might say—some "frenemies." Many Church leaders did not appreciate what a valiant friend and incredible resource they had in Dad. Remember Leonard was censored, spied on, had his projects cancelled, and had Apostles who actively worked to undermine his efforts as Church Historian. What is indicative of Leonard's generous spirit is that in his diary you will find complimentary comments about these very same men's conference sermons. Dad appreciated gospel wisdom and insight even set forth by those very ones who'd clearly meant to do him harm.

Visitors to the Church Historian's Office with Stories to Tell

CARL: People from all walks of life came to visit Leonard in his Church Historian office. Many came because they felt they had experiences or stories to tell that deserved to be preserved for the benefit of the history of the Church. These stories range from the profound to the hilarious. Here is one entitled "Rhoda Carrington's Chair":

> Davis [Bitton] was in this afternoon, and is a good friend of Myra Carrington, granddaughter of Albert Carrington. It appears that Albert's wife, Rhoda Carrington, was very large and obese, [weighing about] 300 pounds. Albert had difficulty getting stockings for her because her [feet were] so small, and her [legs were] so large. He [also] couldn't get a chair which was comfortable for her which she didn't break, so finally, he employed a carpenter to come and make a custom-made chair for her that would be both large enough and strong enough to hold her.

SUSAN: The carpenter needed to have some measurements. She was shy and self-conscious about her weight, and didn't want him to measure her. Finally they devised a stratagem. She would go outside and sit down in the snow bank, and then he would go out and measure the impression she made in the snow. That was done, and she had the chair for the rest of her life.

Leonard's Personal Secretary, Nedra Pace, and Her Story

CARL: Nedra Pace had the opportunity to work as Leonard's personal secretary. She tells the following story that took place in Leonard's office in the east wing of the gleaming, twenty-six story Church Office Building. Here is her story:

> One of the most memorable experiences in working with Dr. Arrington occurred one afternoon when he was working on a long, involved project that had to be out that day. Feeling quite sleepy, he sent me over to Temple View Market to get him a can of Coke, which I carried back unobtrusively in a brown paper bag. I'm sure that this was for purely medicinal purposes. After he had drunk the Coke, he put the can back into the brown paper bag—and stapled it shut—before putting it in the garbage.

Sensitive Information in the Arrington Archive

CARL: Leonard's memory also housed knowledge of many secrets, scandals, misdeeds, and other sensitive information. Much of this knowledge surely died with him in 1999.

There is indeed what some would call sensitive written information in the Leonard Arrington Archive. But, it is not a "warts-and-all" account. There *are* some warts, but because of Leonard's wisdom and sensitivity, there are not nearly as many as there might have been. There are also a few of Leonard's own personal joys, tender moments, and burns and bruises described in his diary.

A Tender Encounter with President Spencer W. Kimball: A Prophet's Kiss

SUSAN: Burns and bruises aside, here is one tender moment experienced during Leonard's service as Church Historian:

> We had a heart-warming experience as we went into the Lion House [for dinner]. President and Sister [Spencer W.] Kimball were just getting out of their car and greeted the three of us very warmly. In fact, President Kimball embraced me and kissed my cheek. He said they very

much appreciated the fine things that we do, and the books we write. He made a little joke about being kept busy just reading our books. He seemed to be in a very good frame of mind. He hung onto me as we walked into the building, and went up the elevator, and down the hall to dinner. His color seemed to be good, and his step rather firm for a person of his age. Camilla, [his wife], was very pleased that we enjoyed her biography.

The Leonard Arrington Archive and Diary Controversy

SUSAN: Some of you here tonight will remember that for a period of time in 2001 and 2002, there was controversy about the contents of Leonard's archival collection housed at USU. Representatives of the LDS Church requested that certain papers given to Leonard when he was Church Historian be returned to the Church and that small, sensitive portions of Leonard's diary be removed before it was open to the public.

In the course of our investigations, the family determined that a small stack of papers, perhaps eight to ten inches high, had been given to Leonard to complete a research project he had been assigned by the First Presidency. After Leonard's death, the Church-owned papers had been inadvertently gathered up and transferred to USU along with tens of thousands of Leonard's own papers. The family happily and voluntarily returned these papers to the Church.

Regarding the requested removal of some of Leonard's diary entries, the family decided that it was best to remove nothing, and to leave the diary as Leonard had written it. Leonard's archival collection, including his diary, is, as we speak, completely intact and available to be read in its entirety at USU Special Collections.

Archive Summary

CARL: Our experience in reading Leonard's diary and his other papers, is that the Leonard Arrington Archives contains many treasures. Buried in his Archive, and someday to be unburied—perhaps by you—are secrets you will find in no other place. There you will find wild tales of the courage and misadventures of trappers, Native American chiefs, governors, ill-fated handcart companies, rich business entrepreneurs, apostles, Danites, FBI intrigue, annoying high school principals, unacknowledged polygamous families, Saints, scholars, and sinners, and people with widely varying degrees of devotion to truth and faith.

Frustrations While Serving as Church Historian

CARL: During Leonard's years as Church Historian and Director of the History Division, he received support and encouragement from many Church officials. But he also experienced significant opposition to his work from some of his supervisors and others holding general Church callings. Knowing this will help us better understand the two diary entries that follow.

SUSAN: The first one is a mock dedication he wrote for his book, *Brigham Young: American Moses*, which was published in 1985, several years after his release as Church Historian. The mock dedication was, of course, never used, and Leonard kept it completely confidential throughout his life. Here it is:

> To Elder Rameumptum J. Moriancumer who, by his regulations and irritating bureaucratic pronouncements, has helped me understand Brigham Young's impatience with self-important people of his own day, thus provoking some of the colorful language which I am delighted to reproduce in this biography.

Another entry is a more personal, more private, and more heart-wrenching summary of Leonard's feelings at the time of his release.

> Our great experiment in Church-sponsored history has proven to be, if not a failure, at least not an unqualified success. One aspect that will be personally galling to me [upon my release as Church Historian] will be the gibes of my non-Mormon and anti-Mormon friends: "I told you so!" [they will say]. Some scholars, Mormons and non-Mormons alike, have contended that skeptical and critical methods of historical research and writing are incompatible with the maintenance of a firm testimony of the Gospel. I have felt confident that they were wrong, and I have said so publicly many times—in professional papers, talks, books, and private conversations."

Leonard's Legacy

Leonard the Humorist: Admiring Precision and Clarity

CARL: After Leonard moved from his office in the Church Office Building in 1982, he continued to be a man who loved precision and clarity, and humor. Consider, for instance, his take on the frustrations of bachelor cooking during the time following the death of our mother,

Grace. Woody Allen has nothing on Leonard as a comedian of the commonplace. Leonard wrote:

> My Stouffer's [cooking] instructions say: "Place chicken pouch on non-metallic plate, and puncture top three to four times with fork, to vent." Well, is it three, or [is it] four? If I puncture it three [times], what might happen? What if I puncture it four? Would it get too much air on four? Would it explode if only three? Why don't they say what they mean? Then it says, "Heat three to four minutes." OK, should it be three, or should it be four? Will it be undercooked if three? Or overcooked at four? Or does it depend on the altitude? And if I am at 4,000 feet, should it be [cooked] three or four [minutes]? I simply can't stand this indefiniteness; it's driving me crazy making these decisions when I am so ignorant and inexperienced!

The madness continues with complexities of garbage day.

> I get a note left by the garbage man, which says that they are not required to take more than six cans of garbage [from my house]. What does that mean? Can I put out six cans plus two boxes? Or do the boxes count as cans? Can I put out six cans and two garbage disposal bags? Or do the latter [also] count as cans? If I leave more than the instructions indicate, will he simply leave the extra ones? Or will he assess a fine? What [exactly] happens? If I leave seven cans and one bag, will the fine be less than if I left eight cans and two bags? It's all so indefinite.

Leonard the Historical Sage

SUSAN: In spite of the changes in his life—his buffeting from previous Church administrators, journalists, and the hazy-minded likes of Mrs. Stouffer—Leonard managed to flourish, publish, and contribute mightily as an historical sage in an uncertain world. After his time as Church Historian, our mother, Grace, died, but his work went on. He published his biography of Brigham Young to great acclaim, survived a sextuple-bypass heart surgery, and was the first Utahn, and first Mormon, to be elected a member of the elite Society of American Historians. He also wrote the definitive history of Idaho, prepared and delivered his brilliant series of Five Lectures on Faith and the Intellect (which was presented in Hawaii), published histories of a linen supply company, the Hotel Utah, the Tracy Collins Bank, and a wonderful biography of Utah's most audacious and colorful cowboy, Charlie Redd. His final book, issued just a few months before his death, was his first book-length biography of a woman, *Madelyn Cannon Stewart Silver: Poet, Teacher, and Homemaker*. And, of course, he told his own story in his memoir, *Adventures of a Church Historian*.

Leonard the Saint

CARL: By the end of his life, Leonard had surely accomplished more than the little Twin Falls farm boy ever dreamed of. He had survived disease, hunger, war, love, fatherhood, PhD oral exams, controversy, and ecclesiastical opposition to his work.

SUSAN: Davis Bitton, assistant Church historian along with Jim Allen, from 1972 to 1982, said:

> Leonard was my closest, dearest friend . . . I was with him almost every day. Leonard loved our Latter-day Saint history and its people, high and low, male and female, Caucasian and non-Caucasian. He wanted to tell our history in a way that would be true to its richness, that would recognize both its wonderful humanity and the divinity that shapes its ends, that would be honest and true and therefore credible.

CARL: The morning of February 11, 1999, Leonard arose early from his bed and tottered out in his pajamas, opened the front door to feel the cold winter air, and picked up the morning edition of *The Salt Lake Tribune*. Perhaps he knew that morning, that it was time. Whatever his thoughts that morning, he left us.

We miss him to this day, yet we happily acknowledge that there are now new winds blowing in regards to the writing of Mormon and Western History that are very much in keeping with the honest and forthright spirit set forth by our father. It is hard to imagine books like Richard Bushman's brilliant *Rough Stone Rolling*, biography of Joseph Smith, and the frank and carefully researched book about the Mountain Meadows Massacre, without the pioneering scholarship of Leonard Arrington.

Leonard's Ecstatic Peak Experience

SUSAN: An historian commits his life to understanding and writing about people and events he is passionate about. The great historians each have their own distinct motivations and inspiration for the work they do. After listening to all of Leonard's accomplishments and wildly-prolific publishing, one might rightfully ask: what motive could drive this particular man to write so many professional books, papers and speeches, to enlighten so many students in so many classes, and in addition, to type out a thirty thousand page diary like Leonard Arrington?

Why? Why? Why? *Why did he* do it?

[LONG PAUSE]

CARL: Actually we *know* why, and Leonard tells the story eloquently. As is appropriate on a night when we honor him, we will give the historian the final word.

> One afternoon, early in 1950, sitting in an alcove of the university library, I had what might be called a "peak experience"—one that sealed my devotion to Latter-day Saint history. Going over my extended notes, recalling the letters, diaries, and personal histories of the hundreds of past church leaders and members, a feeling of ecstasy suddenly came over me—an exhilaration that transported me to a higher level of consciousness. The Apostle John wrote that to gain salvation a person must receive two baptisms—the baptism of water and the baptism of the Spirit (John 3–5). My water baptism and confirmation had occurred when I was eight, but now, in a university library, I was unexpectedly absorbed into the universe of the Holy Spirit . . . A meaningful moment of insight and connectedness had come to me that helped me to see that my research efforts were compatible with the divine restoration of the church. It was something like, but more intense than, the feelings that welled up in me when I listened to the finale of Beethoven's Ninth Symphony or was moved by Raphael's painting of the Madonna in the Vatican museum at the end of World War II. In an electrifying moment, the lives and beliefs of nineteenth-century Mormons had a special meaning; they were inspiring—part of the eternal plan—and it was my pleasure to understand and write about their story. Whatever my talents and abilities—and I had never pretended that they were extraordinary—an invisible higher power had now given me a commission and the experience remained, and continues to remain, with me. Regardless of frustrations and obstacles that came to me in the years that followed, I knew that God expected me to carry out a research program of his peoples' history and to make available that material to others. Whatever people might say about this mortal errand, I must persevere, and do so in an attitude of faithfulness. My experience was a holy, never-to-be-forgotten encounter—one that inspired me to live up to the promises held out for those who receive the gift of the Holy Ghost.